# ADVENT

# Advent

Ripples from Providence

It's not even December, and I can hardly believe it, but I'm sailing into the Christmas season with all my gifts bought and wrapped! The house is fully decorated—I'm talking magazine-worthy—and the pantry is stocked with ingredients to make homemade treats for all my friends and family.

You're right. I'm totally joking. That would be the Shellie of my dreams.

I'm actually reminding myself to take a deep breath and consider what I already know. If I make these holy days about any of those things, I'll miss the joy of the celebration. I'll need to make an intentional decision to place my brown eyes on Jesus—Immanuel, God with Us. And because this has been my goal for several years now, I know something else. I'll need to make that choice more than once during the holiday as the commercialism builds.

Can you relate? Do you want to *live* Christmas instead of *doing* Christmas? Join me, and let's walk through Advent, to-gether. Jesus is worthy.

Hugs,
Shellie

Dec. 1

*Glory to God in the highest, and on earth peace,* good will *to-ward* men. *Luke 2:14*

For believers, the Christmas holiday holds meaning far beyond feel-good movies and familiar carols. We long for our friends and families to experience the glorious present tense impact of Jesus' miraculous birth and embrace the Savior who offers reconciliation between God and men. So, what can we do? We can begin by walking into this holy season realizing that people often experience God through our lives before they ever taste Him for themselves. Instead of wringing our hands over those around us who are missing the glorious message, we can live in a way that spreads it.

It's true, this world is bloated with religion but starved for Jesus. The good news is we can share the Bread of Life with our circles by feeding on His Word ourselves until we leave His table with food to offer people who don't even know they're hungry for it! We can't give our loved ones and communities the joy of the Lord, but we can magnify Him before them by continually looking to Jesus to satisfy our own souls. We can't give a single person the peace that passes understanding. But our lives can so drip with the soul peace we find in Jesus that others begin to seek Him, too.

This Christmas, let's lead the way...

Dec. 2

*But where sin increased, grace abounded all the more …*
*Romans 5:20*

It's going to be impossible not to notice the increasing commercialism of Christmas as the season progresses. We know this. That's why it's such a good and necessary idea to ask the Holy Spirit to help us stay focused on its true meaning. But as we walk through this season, let's make sure our observations about "consumer Christmas" aren't leading us into conversations that could alienate the very ones who need to hear the good news!

Super-abounding grace in the face of very real sin was the glorious reality presented in the garden at sin's initial strike. Promise given even as punishment was handed down. Sin found a place in Eve, spread to Adam, and snared all of humanity, but Grace appeared in the middle of their mess—and He lives in the midst of our sin-reeling consumer driven world, too. This is the news we're meant to share without sticking our heads in the sand and proclaiming all is lost for the rest of the world while "the few, the proud, the saved" live on doctored memories of days gone by. And we can do it, with His help!

Here's to the Good News! Jesus, Immanuel with Us.

Dec. 3

*Behold the lamb of God which taketh away the sin of the world. John 1:29*

The goal of walking through Christmas with our eyes trained on Jesus isn't to make it through the holidays without going straight running crazy (although much can be said for being sane come January). The goal is nothing short of knowing the transformative presence of the Savior the baby was born to be!

God won't drag us into a deep and wide relationship with Him, and we can't find it by trying harder to do better. That's religion, man meeting the bar man sets so man feels good about man. Living life with Christ is as far from such a religious system built on rule-keeping as the east is from the west. Looking to Jesus for salvation is to inherit eternal life. To look again, and again, to live looking at Him instead of us—this is what the Bible calls "beholding" Him. And it's the secret of a life being molded by Christ!

If we'll quit plotting our progress and fix our eyes on Jesus, He'll do the heavy lifting of making us over into His image. Watch for Him with me, today.

Dec. 4

*You will seek Me and find Me, when you seek Me with all of your heart. Jeremiah 29:13*

We can have so much more than a meaningful Christmas. Jesus can form Himself in the Bethlehem of our hearts as surely as He grew up in the ancient city if we'll own our complacency and ask God to turn it into holy hunger.

We are pilgrims, designed for more. In Him we can be satisfied without being settled, loved without being lazy, rest while ever reaching. If we get saved to sit down, we miss the delightful God-designed tension of living in pursuit of an inexhaustible and eternal Savior who satisfies us while creating a hunger for the only more that is forevermore.

The blessing of a life transformed by Christ is never forced on settlers. It's reserved for seekers. Hello seeker, I'm thankful to have you on this journey.

Dec. 5

*Jesus said, "I am the door: by Me if any man enters in, he shall be saved, and shall go in and out, and find pasture." John 10:9*

Believer, beware. It's possible to get so caught up doing Christmas that we resort to coasting on the leftovers of our last devotional or worship service. Whether that be a conscious or unintentional decision, we'll be weaker for it.

Have you settled somewhere between coming to Jesus for eternal life and continuing to come to Him for abundant life? You're not alone, and that's not a good thing. I don't know what's more tragic, that this Door of nourishment and fellowship is undervalued and neglected by unbelievers, or by believers! Believers neglecting the Door, Shellie? Yes. Our dry faith rats us out, and the Word testifies to our malnutrition.

Our invitation is to come to Jesus for eternal life, and our challenge is to keep coming to Him for abundant life.

Dec. 6

*He who loves Me will be loved by My Father, and I will love him and will disclose Myself to him. John 14:21*

Here's a challenge for us all. Let's expect God today to reveal Himself to us. Wherever we are and whatever task we're marking off the Christmas list, let's remind ourselves that God is near, ask Him to speak, and go about our day listening for His Voice in Scripture, in our hearts, and in His creation that surrounds us.

I believe you and I experience God in our daily lives to the degree that we desire and expect to experience God. Our relationship with Him will be as strong or as weak as our determination to know Him beyond the understanding we have when we first believe. Too many of us cede our personal responsibility to seek God to the leadership of our preachers and teachers—and in relinquishing our personal pursuit of God, we relinquish the promise of Christ. Namely, life in His Presence where He regularly discloses Himself to us personally.

Let's have eyes for Jesus today. He is with us.

Dec. 7

*I will establish My covenant between Me and you and your descendants after you throughout their generations for an everlasting covenant, to be God to you and to your descendants after you. Genesis 17:7*

We don't have to participate in the Crazy Christmas Countdown. We can enjoy this day instead of seeing it as one less opportunity to get everything done. Here's an idea: Let's ask God to be God to us today. The very thought brings my blood pressure down, and the idea isn't even mine. It's His!

Over and over in the Scriptures, God expresses His intention to be our God and for us to be His people. The variation of this phrasing I love the most is His often-expressed desire to "be God to you." It's mentioned first in Genesis 17:7. Whatever that fantastic promise includes, it's one of God's go-to expressions. He uses those words or similar phrasing more than three hundred times in His Word.

God has more for all of us, whether we're new followers or mature believers. Today, let's ask the Holy Spirit to help us respond to God's intense love for our company with a passion for His!

Dec. 8

*Teach me your way, O Lord; I will walk in Your truth; unite my heart to fear your name. I will give thanks to You, O Lord my God, with all my heart, and will glorify Your name forever. Psalm 86:11-12*

I need Jesus. You do, too. The truth is, our best intentions to fix our eyes on Jesus and walk through Christmas worshipping Him instead of getting ambushed by the demands of the holiday will fail us without His holy help. Call to Him with me. #911 Jesus, we need you!

As I've confessed, I'm not beyond getting stuck in the muck of me, but I've found that when I live asking the Holy Spirit to alert me to my wrong thinking, He is faithful to do precisely that. He'll do this for you, too. The Spirit of God is ever willing to blow on the fire He started in our hearts, but we must quit trying to stir our lagging passion by working up repentance or charting our obedience.

One of the greatest discoveries of our believing lives is when we realize the hope for our passionless, disjointed, hit-and-miss faith is found in the same One Who gave us the first measure!

Dec. 9

*Out of my distress I called on the Lord; the Lord answered me and set me in a broad place. Psalm 118:5*

Trying to create a wonderful Christmas for someone else wearies the best of us. It's also as futile as trying to earn God's love when we already have it. This season is ours to enjoy, but we can miss it while we work for it! Let's fire ourselves from the impossible job of making Christmas happen and let Jesus rule the day.

There's no comparison between that life of striving and the one where we trust Jesus to deliver us from the power of sin the same way He delivered us from its guilt! It's why I ask Him to boss me as soon as I open my eyes in the morning! I know that if I'm not obeying Him, I'll be trying to rule. Praise God, we're free from striving when He is governing.

Far from living a narrow life of do's and don'ts, dying to live leaves us standing in the deep and wide expanse of His love. Say it with me, *Boss me, Jesus. I am yours.*

Dec. 10

*Then Jesus declared, "I am the Bread of Life." John 6: 25*

What is sustaining you this Christmas? And I'm not talking about coffee and chocolate versus smoothies and kale. (I know where I fall on that one!) This is a reminder that what we're depending on or Who we're drawing from is obvious to those around us.

It's called a food chain. We've heard of them, but do we realize we're passing on what we're feeding on? Genesis tells us that once Eve ate, she gave to her husband, and he ate. That's sobering. It means the conclusions we draw about what is good for food, lovely to behold, and desirable to make us wise— (conclusions Eve drew!)— have impact far beyond our individual choices. It may not be today, and it may not be to-morrow, but those dearest to us will benefit from being in our food chain, or they'll pay the cost of us finding our nourishment and satisfaction outside of God.

What will we choose for ourselves, and for those we love today?

Dec. 11

*Cry aloud and shout thy inhabitant of Zion, for great in your midst is the Holy One of Israel. Isaiah 12:6*

There is more hope available to us today. There is more peace, more comfort, more joy, more of everything we need. God is at hand, offering more of Himself than any of us have experienced. Let's reach for Him.

God's invitation is so much bigger than mere rescue because life is God's idea, and He wants to experience it with us. You and I were never meant to travel through this world without His Presence, toughing it out all by our lonesome. Our good Father intended to share our waking-up, sitting-down, pleasant, painful, joyful, mournful, exhilarating, and exhausting moments. He longs for us to see they're all holy moments. Don't let the word "holy" throw you. I want to encourage you to begin enlarging your idea of holiness, of what is sacred and what isn't. Forget the religious notions that come to mind when you hear the word and consider this instead:

Every moment spent with God is holy because God is holy, and wherever we are, He is.

Dec. 12

*For this is eternal life, that they might know you, the only true God, and Jesus Christ whom You have sent. John 17:3*

Enjoy the season. Give and receive with joy. But keep in mind even must-have gifts eventually lose their appeal and sought-after experiences fall short of expectations. There's only One who will always be more than we are longing for—His name is Jesus.

With Jesus, there are no diminishing returns; just divine, compelling answers to our deepest desires to know and be known. He satiates our soul while stirring our longing. In Him we find contentment laced with longing, satisfaction colored with the sweetest hunger. Strange? Yes. Otherworldly? Yes. That's Jesus.

Ever-increasing joy and satisfaction lie in Jesus because in Him we taste the first course of eternity.
Hugs,

Dec. 13



*Mercy triumphs over judgment. James 2:13*

The perfect Christmas will never be found in the decorations, the gifts, or the food, but in a sincere celebration of the day Heaven's King came to earth with baby fingers and baby toes. Ponder His purpose and worship: This holy child was born to die that fallen us might live.

Grab a scrap of paper and print this next line out where you can see it today and tomorrow. Put it on your refrigerator. Write it with lipstick on your bathroom mirror. Do whatever you need to do to hold on to it. "Man's sin against God did not extinguish God's love for man. It never does." So, tell me. Have you taken some bad roads, made some poor choices? You're still ridiculously loved by God, as demonstrated through Christ Jesus.

You haven't worn out God's great love. He is long-suffering and He is for you.

Dec. 14

*But if we walk in the light as He Himself is in the light, we have fellowship with one another and the blood of Jesus His Son cleanses us from all sin. 1 John 1:7*

We're two weeks into December, and despite our sincere intentions, there's a chance you and I have already lost the Christmas spirit once, if not a couple times. Am I right? If that's you, let's ask forgiveness and train our eyes back on Jesus! His company will be our reward!

Being all too aware of how often we fall short of holy, it's hard for us to believe we can dwell with God all day every day, and in His favor no less. But we must remind ourselves of this truth because if we aren't convinced that we're being cleansed, just as we have been cleansed, the enemy will continue to cheat us of the joy of walking in friendship with Jesus on this side of Heaven.

Truth says we live in God's favor through our faith in Christ's finished work, and we can't hear that often enough. Let's remind ourselves of this soul-nourishing reality today, and then, let's tell someone else who needs to hear it, too!

Dec. 15

*Take My yoke upon you and learn from Me, for I am gentle and humble in heart, and you will find rest for your souls. Matthew 11:29*

Pause and reach for the marvelous opportunity that is ours to walk with the God of the whole universe today. Through Christ Jesus, we can come before Him without intricate steps, fancy prayer words, or prescribed formulas. That's the Gospel. That's the good news.

Whether or not we build our lives into a home where God is welcomed, and His Presence is enjoyed will depend on whether we voluntarily lay the building blocks of our lives before Him. Believers who never experience the intimate friendship with God provided by Jesus have failed to understand such relationship isn't a given or a duty, but a privilege.

We don't have to build our lives into a sanctuary...We get to!

Dec. 16

*Here I am! I stand at the door and knock. If anyone hears my voice and opens the door, I will come in and eat with that person, and they with me. Revelation 3:20*

Sweet believer, you who came once for salvation. You say you don't know how to come to Jesus for day-to-day life? It's easier than your enemy would have you believe. Acknowledge His reign, submit your will, and then use your words to bring Him anything and everything, anytime and all the time.

Every day, all day, we're given opportunities to cling to our right to ourselves or concede everything we are in voluntary offerings to everything He is. It's our privilege to bring God our eyes, ears, words, desires, thoughts, actions, goals, priorities, and intentions, and these choices build our lives into His dwelling place where He will meet with us, where He will speak to us. Granted, that's not an exhaustive list. It's an idea of the materials within reach of us all that can hinder our walk with God or build Him a home in our nine-to-fives.

Might I give you a message from Jesus? "Welcome home."

Dec. 17

*For by grace you have been saved through faith; and that not of yourselves, it is the gift of God. Ephesians 2:8*

People are prone to making us perform to stay in their good graces or do penance if we let them down. We lose big when we allow those experiences to color our relationship with God. No amount of penance before God can secure the favor Christ Jesus has already won on our behalf.

I've learned to live celebrating the truth that I'm forgiven, accepted, and loved when I feel like it—and when I don't. I've discovered the power of reminding myself Jesus not only met the bar for me; He obliterated the measuring stick. I delight in reminding myself I'm not poked and prodded and scrutinized for admission at the Door. I'm warmly welcomed and fully received through Christ Jesus.

And the very best news of the season, friend? It's true for you, too!

Dec. 18

*I am the vine, you are the branches; he who abides in Me and I in him, he bears much fruit, for apart from Me you can do nothing. John 15:5*

Christmas may be drawing closer, but for those who have trusted Christ, its promise is already ours! We can say no to the commercialism with its empty promise of the perfect Christmas by saying yes to Immanuel, God with Us, the perfect Savior.

We don't want to try harder to do better, remember? We want to lean harder, and trust Jesus to strengthen our dusty frames from the inside out. We're learning to say yes and amen to Jesus's word, "Without me you can do nothing!" We're learning we can't manage our sins through the strength of our willpower and we're learning to rely on Jesus to make us victorious over them.

Trying harder is religion's trap. It's fueled by fear and guilt, and it will fail us every time, but abounding joy is the delightful surprise of grace-driven obedience. Selah.

Dec. 19

*For with You is the fountain of life; in Your light we see light.*
*Psalm 36:9*

The Christmas countdown may bring stressful shopping trips and exchanges with the occasional grumpy grinch, but you and I are not only called to be Christlike in our response, we're equipped for it. Immanuel is real world support for all who learn to call on Him.

I haven't yet made it to a place where I'm always saintly, and I don't live with unlimited patience for those around me. The soul-enriching difference for me is that I now understand how quickly darkness can creep in and consume my thoughts if I refuse to expose them to the Light. And I've discovered the immeasurable benefit of owning up to how much I need Jesus and asking Him for help over, again, and constantly. I can't recommend this life of running to Jesus strongly enough.

When we openly acknowledge our inability to live for Jesus without drawing from Jesus, we get to pull from the bottomless well of resources that are ours in and through Him! Oh, come let us adore Him...

Dec. 20

*Come, all you who are thirsty, come to the waters; and you who have no money, come, buy and eat! Come, buy wine and milk without money and without cost. Why spend money on what is not bread, and your labor on what does not satisfy? Isaiah 55:1*

Caution. We are the most susceptible to reaching for the wrong fix when we're tired and stressed. Jesus is near, count Him dear and choose well today.

Temporary hits can't satisfy eternal hunger … Whatever we reach for to make ourselves feel better today will become a fix we'll need more of tomorrow. No amount of acquisitions, affirmations, or acclamations from creation can substitute for the Creator. We were created for God, and living for ourselves will always leave us empty.

Jesus is the One we're longing for, and life is found in taking our cavernous souls to Him for filling. Go tell it on the mountain, Jesus Christ is born!

Dec. 21

*But as many as received Him, to them He gave the right to become children of God, even to those who believe in His name, who were born, not of blood nor of the will of the flesh nor of the will of man, but of God. John 1: 12-13*

Sadly, some will be disappointed in their Christmas this year. It's just a fact. Here's an immeasurably better one: The believer's birthright is to have an ever-increasing hunger for God and His Word, and none will be disappointed who refuse to settle for anything less.

I want to whet your appetites with the possibilities of a deep and wide life in Christ. The promise of the Gospel is that every single one of us can enjoy intimacy with God through Christ. We can all come to a place where we crave God's Word instead of resigning ourselves to reading it when we can because we know we should. Every single one of us can come to love and live on prayer instead of going through the motions out of dry commitment. This is our birthright as believers.

Glory to God in the highest, peace on earth, good will to men.

Dec. 22

*Again Jesus said, "Simon son of John, do you truly love me?"
He answered, "Yes Lord, you know that I love you." Jesus said,
"Take care of my sheep." John 21:16*

The to-do list is long, and time seems short, but we walk
among souls our God dearly loves. Our opportunity is to stay
conscious of Jesus and let Him reach for them through our
lives, even as we go about our day.

We don't learn such living in a once and done. We learn it by
daring to die to us and live to Him in this moment and the next,
until we realize Jesus is taking our bloated, self-centered lives
and giving them purpose and meaning. When Jesus becomes
our food, He becomes our life, and our life in Him becomes our
conversation, and in tending others, we keep finding the way
forward. The life He pours into us pours out of us because we
can't contain Him.

Make no mistake, the Spirit in us yearns to make us broken
bread and poured-out wine. Let's yield to Him today.

.

Dec. 23

*He who loves Me will be loved by My Father, and I will love him and will disclose Myself to him. John 14:21*

Christmas is near, and I hope you and yours enjoy every minute of it! My prayer is that these short devotions have set us up to resist the empty promises the world hawks twenty-four/seven and walk into the deep and wide life Jesus died to give us.

It's impossible to read John without wondering about the discrepancy between the experience of the average believer and the one Jesus promised, the one I'm daring us to pursue! We can ignore those words and make excuses for why we're not experiencing them. Or we can quit letting the faith of those around us set the bar for our walk with God and refuse to settle for anything less than what He promised in His Word.

We can pay less attention to what man says about God and more attention to what God says about men. *Lord, grant us ears to hear...*

Dec. 24

*So then, death is at work in us, but life in you! 2 Corinthians 12:4*

If these devotions have stirred you to want more of God, to behold Jesus until He transforms you, tell your family and friends about your intentions. Your experience may just lead them to Christ's life-changing work in their own lives.

Transformation is powerful stuff! The culture knows it—hence the bombardment of before-and-after images in magazines and on home-improvement shows. This transformative life is our calling, and Paul encourages us to live it in Christ transparently! This is why I'm asking us to be brave enough to let others follow our journey. It costs us to let others see our weaknesses, but it encourages them when they see Christ at work in us in those very things. Whether we choose to only show our strengths, or only reveal our weaknesses, either way we fail those watching.

One more Christmas Eve thought? Jesus is the most real to us and through us when we risk what someone may think of us for the greater goal of having them think about Him.

Dec. 25

*For this is eternal life, that they might know you, the only true God, and Jesus Christ whom You have sent. John 17:3*

Merry Christmas, friends! May the love of God, the grace of Christ Jesus and the fellowship of Holy Spirit overwhelm you with joy today. Our devotional has drawn to a close, but I hope you'll stay connected. I want to keep walking forward with you. As Oswald Chambers once said in one of my all-time favorite quotes, "Let the past sleep, but let it sleep on the bosom of Christ. Leave the Irreparable Past in His hands and step out into the Irresistible Future with Him."

Knowing God is our best life because knowing God is Life, and when we set out to know God, we run headlong into His desire to be known. God loves first and best. Believing He is wooing us changes everything. The determined seeker can never want more of God than He is willing to give of Himself.

The love of God is immeasurable and inexhaustible, and He alone mines miracles out of messes. Selah.

Hugs,
Shellie

Selections of this Advent devotional have been taken from Finding Deep and Wide/Salem Books 2020, available for purchase online and wherever books are sold.